This Book Belongs To:

....

To Mum,
Thank you for always supporting me x

First published in paperback in 2024.

Printed in the United Kingdom.

ISBN: 978-1-0369-0732-7

www.elianawantstofly.co.uk

ELIANA WANTS TO FLY

Written by
Maya Komolafe

Illustrated by
Esila Karakuyu

Eliana wants to fly, like
a bird soaring through
the sky.

She wants to fly towards
the sun that's so high!

She wants to travel all around the world, to every country and city.

She wants to fly from Tokyo all the way to Mississippi.

She wants to fly through
the clouds: soft, fluffy
and white.

Yearning to touch them in
the midst of her flight.

She wants to gaze at the sunset in awe of its beauty.

Mesmerised by the iridescent colours as she flies across Djibouti.

She wants to fly higher than the mountains and skyscrapers too.

She'd be far above the ground and she'd love the view.

As she flies past Antigua,
she'll see the dolphins below.

She'll greet them with a smile
and wave them hello.

She wants to fly
amongst the stars as
they glisten and gleam.

And she'd be so happy
because she's living her
dream.

She wants to cross the big oceans so vast and blue.

She wants to cross deserts, rainforests and see the pyramids too.

She'll fly through
thunder, storm and
lightning.

And she'll be brave even
though it may be
frightening.

She'll fly when it's thick
with snow or pouring
with rain.

But she'll be perfectly
fine, she'll never think
to complain.

She wants to glide through
the air so swift
and smooth.

She has a strong desire
that simply can't
be removed.

Eliana wants to fly and
she can hardly wait.

But for now she'll keep on
dreaming until she fulfils
her fate.

About the Author

Maya Komolafe

Maya began writing this book at 17 years old, her passion for writing poems began at a young age. Aspiring to be a commercial airline pilot, Maya hopes Eliana's story will inspire the younger generation to dream big and pursue their ambitions relentlessly.

About the Illustrators

Esila Karakuyu
Illustrator

Yashini Nadeesha
Digital Illustrator

Esila is a 13-year-old with a passion for art. From a young age, she has always been drawing or painting to enhance her skills and still continues to this day. Esila aspires to continue illustrating books and pursue a career in the art industry.

Yashini is a 25-year-old digital illustrator who devotes her career to crafting vibrant worlds for children. She aims to create a sense of joy in every young viewer as they embark on an exciting journey with each captivating illustration.

www.ingramcontent.com/pod-product-compliance
Lightning Source LLC
Chambersburg PA
CBHW042131030726
47599CB00002B/435